Aslan

Cameron

Please Enjoy reading

Pat

Peace

UNIQUE ANIMALS OF THE ISLANDS

By Tanya Lee Stone

BLACKBIRCH PRESS
An imprint of Thomson Gale, a part of The Thomson Corporation

Detroit • New York • San Francisco • San Diego • New Haven, Conn. • Waterville, Maine • London • Munich

For my sister Laurie, my Island Girl!

© 2005 Thomson Gale, a part of The Thomson Corporation.

Thomson and Star Logo are trademarks and Gale and Blackbirch Press are registered trademarks used herein under license.

For more information, contact
Blackbirch Press
27500 Drake Rd.
Farmington Hills, MI 48331-3535
Or you can visit our Internet site at http://www.gale.com

ALL RIGHTS RESERVED.
No part of this work covered by the copyright hereon may be reproduced or used in any form or by any means—graphic, electronic, or mechanical, including photocopying, recording, taping, Web distribution, or information storage retrieval systems—without the written permission of the publisher.

Every effort has been made to trace the owners of copyrighted material.

Cover © Stephen Frank/CORBIS; page 3 © John Banagan/Lonely Planet Images; pages 4 (map), 5 (map) Steve Zmina; pages 4, 5, 20 Corel Corporation; page 6 © Clive Druett; Padillo/CORBIS; page 7 (main) © Robert Pickett/CORBIS; page 7 (inset) Courtesy of the United States Fish and Wildlife Service; pages 8, 10, 11 (main), 18 © Kevin Shafer/CORBIS; page 9 © Greg Lasley; page 11 (inset) © Michael & Patricia Fogden/CORBIS; page 12 © Kennan Ward/CORBIS; page 13 © Wolfgang Kaehler/CORBIS; page 14 © Reuters/CORBIS; page 15 (main) © Gary Braasch/CORBIS; page 16 © Martin Harvey; page 18 © Mark Webster/Lonely Planet Images; page 19 (bottom) © Casey & Astrid Witte Mahaney/Lonely Planet Images; page 19 (top) © Tom Boyden/Lonely Planet Images; page 21 (left) © Tim Rock/Lonely Planet Images; page 21 (right) © David Bryant/Lonely Planet Images; page 22 © Richard Seaman; page 23 (both) Merlin B. Tuttle, Bat Conservation International

LIBRARY OF CONGRESS CATALOGING-IN-PUBLICATION DATA

Stone, Tanya Lee.
    Unique animals of the islands / by Tanya Lee Stone.
       p. cm. — (Regional wild America)
Includes bibliographical references
ISBN 1-4103-0446-9 (hardcover: alk. paper)
    1. Island animals—United States—Insular possessions—Juvenile literature. I. Title II. Series: Stone, Tanya Lee. Regional wild America.
QL155.S759 2005
591.752'0973—dc22

2004011506

Printed in the United States of America
10 9 8 7 6 5 4 3 2 1

Contents

Introduction 4
Leapin' Lizards! 6
Puerto Rican Parrots 8
Croaking Coquis! 10
Big Bird 12
Land of the Leatherback 14
Coconut Crabs 16
Hooray for Hawksbills! 18
Biggest Bivalve 20
Beautiful Bats 22
Glossary 24
For More Information 24
Index 24

Introduction

There are many islands that belong to the United States. Puerto Rico and the U.S. Virgin Islands are in the Atlantic Ocean. Guam, American Samoa, and the Northern Mariana Islands lie in the Pacific Ocean. And there are other small Pacific islands that are part of the U.S. Fish and Wildlife Service's National Wildlife Refuge.

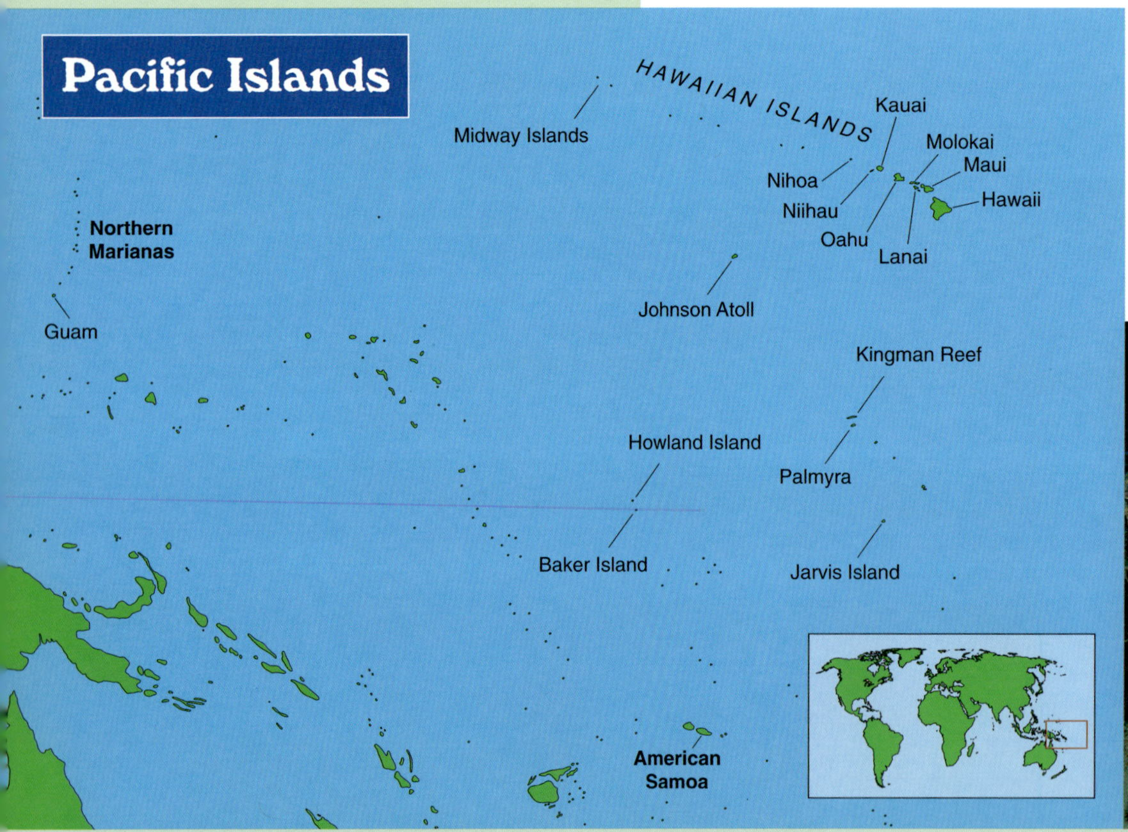

Atlantic Islands

Throughout these islands, birds fly, marine life swims, and animals travel across the land. Many different animals make their homes here. Some animals are especially well known on these islands.

Many unique animals like the hawksbill sea turtle (opposite) and frigate bird (above, left) live throughout the islands of the United States.

Leapin' Lizards!

Horned iguanas are endangered. These iguanas are named for the hornlike scale on their snout. Both males and females have them. A few thousand of these lizards live on Mona Island, off the coast of Puerto Rico. (Mona Island belongs to Puerto Rico.) Mona Island iguanas are quite large, stretching nearly 2 feet (0.6m) in length, not including the tail. Their tails can easily add another 2 feet (0.6m) to their overall length. These iguanas often weigh more than 20 pounds (9kg). They have strong legs and powerful tails.

Iguanas are cold-blooded. When they need to cool their bodies down, they look for shade. When they need to warm up, they bask in the Sun. Mona Island iguanas are diurnal animals. This means they are active during the day. They feed mainly on fruits and flowers. Sometimes they eat caterpillars or crabs. When nighttime comes, they disappear into burrows. They might also

The horned iguana has a hornlike scale on its snout that gives the big lizard its name.

rest in a cave, hollow log, or space under a rock. These iguanas defend their territory from others. They stare down, push, or even try to bite an invader.

Another endangered lizard in this region is the St. Croix ground lizard. This lizard has a small body that stretches about 2 to 3 inches (5 to 8cm). It has stripes that run the length of its body and a ringed tail. It is active during the day and eats ants, sand fleas, white moths, and hermit crabs. There are only about three thousand of these animals left. They are protected at the Green Cay refuge off the coast of St. Croix.

Iguanas feed in the day and find a safe place to rest at night (top). The St. Croix ground lizard (bottom) is also active during the day.

Puerto Rican Parrots

Five hundred years ago, there were not many people in Puerto Rico. But Puerto Rican parrots lived all over the island. There were hundreds of thousands of these birds. Then the numbers of people grew. People cleared forests and took over more of the land. By the 1950s, there were only about two hundred parrots left. Today, there are only about forty of them in the wild. They are in danger of becoming extinct. In fact, the Puerto Rican parrot is one of the ten most endangered birds in the world.

These parrots are 11 to 12 inches (28 to 30cm) long and weigh about 10 ounces (284g). They are very colorful. A Puerto Rican parrot's body is bright green. It has red feathers on its forehead and blue on its wings. White feathers make a ring around its eye. This bird eats mainly fruit and also some flowers and shoots.

Human population growth has pushed the Puerto Rican parrot to near extinction, leaving only about forty birds in the wild.

The Puerto Rican parrot is loud and makes a range of squawking sounds. Sometimes it sounds almost like a bugle! These birds tend to make a lot of noise at dawn. The Puerto Rican parrot makes its nest in a large, deep hole it finds in a Colorado tree. It cleans out the hole but does not add anything to line it. A female lays two to four eggs. These parrots once lived in many kinds of Puerto Rican forests. Today, they are only found in the highland forests where the Colorado trees still grow.

Another bird native to Puerto Rico is also endangered. It is the Puerto Rican yellow-shouldered blackbird. As its name describes, this is a glossy black bird with yellow feathers on its shoulders. Both the yellow-shouldered blackbird and the Puerto Rican parrot are protected. Scientists hope one day there will be many more of them.

The endangered Puerto Rican yellow-shouldered blackbird (pictured) and the Puerto Rican parrot are both protected.

Croaking Coquis!

The coqui tree frog of Puerto Rico sings from sundown to sunup.

What is as big as your thumbnail and sings all night? A coqui tree frog! These tiny frogs are native to Puerto Rico. There are several different kinds of coquis. A few of them may be extinct. Others are either rare or endangered. These frogs have large toe pads. They can be green, brown, or yellow. They vary a bit in size, too. Some are less than 1 inch (2.5cm) long, while others grow to be about 3 inches (8cm) in length.

Like all frogs, the coqui is an amphibian. But one of the unique things about coqui frogs is that they do not have a tadpole stage of life. That means their eggs do not need to be laid in water. Instead, the mother coqui carries her eggs until they are ready to hatch into little frogs. The golden coqui actually gives birth to live young!

Coqui frogs make a high-pitched sound—ko-kee—that can be heard through the night in Puerto Rico. They begin to sing when the Sun goes down and they do not stop until it rises in the morning. The males sing to attract females and to mark territory. The coqui frog is an important symbol in Puerto Rico. It appears in paintings, songs, and other works of Puerto Rican art.

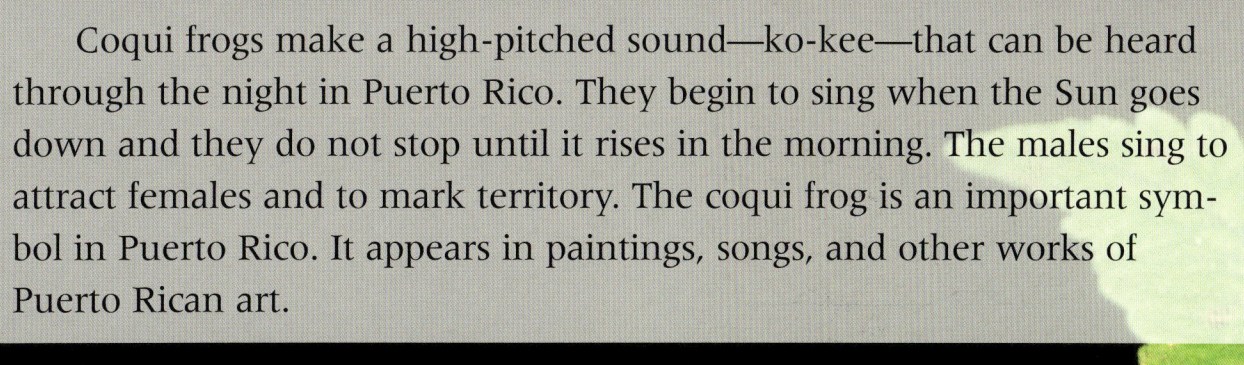

Unlike most frogs, a mother coqui carries her eggs (inset) until they develop into baby frogs, allowing her to give birth away from water.

Big Bird

The magnificent frigate bird is well named. It is an awesome sight. A frigate bird has a long, hooked bill. Its long tail is forked at the end. And its large wings are pointed at the tips. The bird's body feathers are black. Males have a red throat sac that they puff out when trying to attract females. Females have white breasts.

This large bird is more than 40 inches (102cm) long. Its wings spread more than 7 feet (2m). Frigate birds often glide for hours. They have short legs and little feet. This makes it difficult for them to land. Although they are seabirds, they never land on the water. To rest, they often land in trees or on rocks.

Two male frigate birds show their red throat sacs during breeding season. Though they are seabirds, they often land in trees.

These birds do not dive down into the water either. To catch a fish, a frigate bird flies just above the surface and quickly snatches up its prey. They are good at catching flying fish as these fish launch themselves in and out of the water. Frigate birds get a lot of their meals by chasing other birds away from food so they can steal it.

Frigate birds that are not breeding often fly along both coasts of the United States. But they nest in large groups, or colonies, in the Florida Keys and in the U.S. Virgin Islands. A male and female pair builds a nest as a team. The male collects the materials and the female builds the nest. A female frigate bird lays only one egg during a breeding season. It takes about fifty days for the egg to hatch. Both parents care for the egg and the newly born chick.

Male frigate birds puff out their red throat pouches to attract female attention.

Land of the Leatherback

As their name suggests, sea turtles live in the sea. But their eggs are laid on land. Some hawksbill and green turtles nest around Puerto Rico and the U.S. Virgin Islands. But leatherback turtles make up the biggest number of nesting sea turtles in this area. The Sandy Point National Wildlife Refuge on the island of St. Croix offers leatherbacks a protected environment. Leatherbacks also nest on certain beaches on St. John and Puerto Rico.

Most turtles have hard shells. But the leatherback gets its name from the leathery skin that covers it. The leatherback is the biggest of all turtles. A leatherback can weigh more than 1,000 pounds (454kg) and stretch more than 8 feet (2m) in length! These animals are fast, strong swimmers and move easily through the water.

Every two or three years, a female comes on land to nest. To do this, she has to haul her heavy body out of the sea. She climbs slowly onto the beach and looks for a good spot. She uses her back flippers to dig a hole in the sand. Then she lays about eighty eggs into it. With both her front and back flippers, she carefully covers the eggs with sand. This protects them from the weather, and from animals that would eat them.

Once the nest is safely covered, the female heads back into the ocean. She does not stay to care for the eggs or the hatchlings that will crawl out of the nest about sixty-five days later. The baby turtles must make their way out of the nest and into the ocean by themselves.

Volunteers check this leatherback turtle's health (left). Females pull themselves onto land to lay eggs (pictured). A hatchling (inset) must find its way to the ocean on its own.

Coconut Crabs

An atoll is a ring-shaped island or group of tiny islands that protect reefs and shallow water. In the Pacific Ocean, the Palmyra Atoll is a group of about fifty tiny islands and reefs. It lies about halfway between California and Australia.

There are no people living here. But the Palmyra Atoll is home to a huge variety of life and more kinds of coral than almost anywhere else on earth. Palmyra is a resting place for more than 1 million seabirds throughout the year.

One unique creature that lives on Palmyra is the coconut crab. It is the largest land invertebrate in the world. These crabs weigh up to 10 pounds (4.5kg) and live up to fifty years. Their legs can stretch more than 2 feet (0.6m) in length. Coconut crabs have extremely sharp and powerful claws. They can actually take the husk off of a coconut and get to the meat and milk inside. These crabs even climb trees to reach their favorite food!

Coconut crabs use their strong claws to climb trees (opposite). The crab at right climbs a coconut palm in search of its favorite food.

Hooray for Hawksbills!

A hawksbill turtle searches a Pacific reef for something tasty to eat.

Hawksbill sea turtles are one of seven kinds of sea turtles. They swim in warm waters throughout the world. Hawksbills are seen around the coral reefs off the Pacific islands of Hawaii, Guam, American Samoa, and the Northern Marianas. They are also found in the waters off of smaller Pacific islands such as Palmyra Atoll.

Hawksbills weigh between 100 and 200 pounds (45 to 91kg). Their shells grow to a length of about 3 feet (0.9m). Hawksbills can swim up to 15 miles (24km) per hour. When females are ready to lay their eggs, they come out of the water. A female hawksbill will climb onto the beach once every two to five years to lay her eggs. She digs a nesting pit and lays 150 to 180 eggs. Females use their flippers to cover the eggs with dirt. The eggs hatch about sixty days later. The hatchlings scramble down the beach to get into the water as fast as they can.

A man releases an endangered hawksbill back into the ocean (right), saving it from being eaten or used for jewelry. The hawksbill gets its name from its sharp beak (below).

The hawksbill sea turtle gets its name from its hooked beak. This hard beak serves the turtle well as it looks for food in the sharp nooks and crannies of a coral reef. Hawksbills love to eat sea sponges. They also eat sea urchins, algae, and jellyfish. To get rid of the salt from the ocean water they drink, these turtles cry big salty tears!

The number of hawksbills is dropping fast. More than 1 million hawksbill turtles have been killed since 1970. Their meat and their eggs are used for food. Most hawksbills are killed for their shells. A turtle's top shell is called its carapace. The carapace is made of overlapping pieces called scutes. A hawksbill's thick scutes have a beautiful pattern. The term "tortoise shell" was often used for scutes that came from a hawksbill shell. People have made jewelry, hair clips, combs, boxes, and other objects from them. Today, hawksbills are endangered.

Biggest Bivalve

Giant clams are found in the Pacific and Indian oceans. In keeping with their name, these clams grow to 5 feet (1.5m) across and can weigh up to 550 pounds (250kg). The giant clam is the largest bivalve in the world. (A bivalve is a soft-bodied animal without a skeleton. Its shell has two halves.)

They are long-lived creatures. They live up to one hundred years! Giant clams are too large and heavy to swim around in the water. They stay in one spot on the coral reefs where they live. But they do open and close their thick, heavy shells. Once they are fully grown, giant clams are not able to completely close their shells.

The beautifully colored giant clam is the world's largest bivalve. Algae live inside the clams, providing food and requiring the clams to live in sunlight.

Their main source of food comes from tiny algae that live inside the clam. The algae produce sugars that are taken in by the clam. In return, the clam protects the algae from predators. This kind of relationship in which

both animals need each other to survive is called symbiotic. Giant clams are not found in water deeper than 65 feet (20m). That is because the algae that lives in the giant clam need sunlight to grow.

Giant clams are beautifully colored. They have spots of purple, blue, or green around the edges of their mantles. Sometimes there are so many of these spots that the color looks solid.

Beautiful Bats

An animal called a flying fox lives on the islands of American Samoa. But it is not a fox at all. It is a fruit bat! Samoan flying foxes mainly eat fruit. They also like sap, nectar, and pollen.

Bats are special because they are the only kind of mammal that can fly. Samoan flying foxes glide through the air with wingspans of more than 3 feet (0.9 m). They weigh between 14 to 18 ounces (400 to 500g).

Unlike many kinds of bats, flying foxes do not roost in large groups. They hang from branches alone, or as a pair. A mother will also roost with her young. Thousands of these flying foxes were killed by hunters in the 1980s. Today, it is illegal to hunt them.

On the islands of Guam and the Marianas, another fruit bat is in trouble. On Guam, the Mariana fruit bat was widely hunted for food. Many are also eaten by brown tree snakes. The Mariana fruit bat is now endangered on Guam and protected locally on the other islands.

An endangered Samoan flying fox enjoys a meal of pandanus fruit.

Like the Samoan flying fox, this bat has a wingspan of more than 3 feet (1 m). Its body and wings are a darkish brown. The sides of its neck are golden. During the day, groups of these bats spend a lot of time sleeping. After the sun sets, they take off to find food. They eat many different kinds of fruits, including papayas, figs, and breadfruit. They also love flowers.

There are many unique and wonderful animals that live in and around American islands. They all add to the richness and beauty of these places.

A Mariana fruit bat snacks on a flower. Mariana fruit bats have foxlike faces (inset).

Glossary

Bivalve A soft-bodied animal that has a shell with two halves and no skeleton.
Carapace The top of a turtle's shell.
Diurnal Asleep at night and active during the day.
Invertebrate An animal that has no backbone.
Mantle A fleshy fold of tissue that encloses the internal organs.
Omnivore An animal that eats plants and other animals.
Scute The scaly covering of a turtle's shell.

For More Information

Lee Jacobs, *Crow* (Wild America series). San Diego, CA: Blackbirch Press, 2003.

Bobbie Kalman. *The Life Cycle of a Sea Turtle*. New York: Crabtree, 2002.

Sandra Markle. *Outside and Inside Bats*. New York: Atheneum, 1997.

Tanya Lee Stone. *Lizards* (Wild Wild World series). San Diego, CA: Blackbirch Press, 2003.

Index

American Samoa, 4, 18, 22
Amphibian, 10
Atoll, 16

Bats, 22–23
Birds, 8–9, 12–13
Bivalves, 20–21

Clams, 20–21
Coconut crabs, 16–17
Cold-blooded animals, 6
Coqui tree frog, 10–11
Coral, 17
Crabs, 16–17

Eggs, 10, 13, 14–15, 18

Endangered species, 6, 7, 8, 9, 10, 19, 22
Extinction, 8, 10

Flying fox, 22–23
Flying mammals, 22
Frigate bird, 12–13
Frogs, 10–11

Giant clams, 20–21
Guam, 4, 18, 22

Hawksbill sea turtles, 14, 18–19

Iguanas, 6–7

Leatherback turtles, 14–15
Lizards, 6–7

Nests, 13, 14–15, 18
Northern Mariana Islands, 4, 18, 22

Palmyra Atoll, 16–17, 18
Parrots, 8–9
Puerto Rican parrots, 8–9
Puerto Rican yellow-shouldered blackbird, 9
Puerto Rico, 4, 6, 10–11, 14

Reefs, 16, 18, 19, 20

Seabirds, 12, 17
Sea turtles, 14–15, 18–19
St. Croix ground lizard, 7
Symbiotic relationship, 21

Tree frogs, 10–11
Turtles, 14–15, 18–19

U.S. Virgin Islands, 4, 13, 14

Wings, 12, 22, 23

Yellow-shouldered blackbird, 9